# Professor Science

## AND THE SALAMANDER STUMPER

by Donna Latham
illustrated by Bill Petersen

PEARSON

Scott
Foresman

Editorial Offices: Glenview, Illinois • Parsippany, New Jersey • New York, New York
Sales Offices: Needham, Massachusetts • Duluth, Georgia • Glenview, Illinois
Coppell, Texas • Ontario, California • Mesa, Arizona

Every effort has been made to secure permission and provide appropriate credit for photographic material. The publisher deeply regrets any omission and pledges to correct errors called to its attention in subsequent editions.

Unless otherwise acknowledged, all photographs are the property of Scott Foresman, a division of Pearson Education.

Illustrations by Bill Petersen

ISBN: 0-328-13471-6

4 5 6 7 8 9 10  V0G1  14 13 12 11 10 09 08 07 06

My mom has one of the wildest jobs in the world. It is conveniently located just a few blocks away from my school. Every day after middle school lets out, my big sister, Nicole, walks over to pick up my younger sister, Sophie, and me at Robert Frost Elementary School. Then we rush over to Mom's work. You never know what we'll discover—a lion with a sore tooth or baboons having a ball.

Like I said, Mom's job is wild! She's the zookeeper at Lakemoor Zoo. When I grow up, I want to be a scientist, like Mom. I love to hang around the zoo and learn all kinds of scientific stuff. I have a special notebook Mom gave me to record all my observations. I never go anywhere without it.

When Nicole came to pick us up today, she was waving a note Mom had tucked into her lunch.

"Doug! Sophie!" she called. "Mom has some exciting news to tell us when we get to the zoo."

"I wonder what it is," said Sophie. "Maybe some little koala babies were born, or the dolphins learned some new tricks."

"I'll bet a new animal's arriving at the Herpetology House," I said. Herpetology is the study of reptiles and amphibians, and the Herpetology House is my very favorite place in the whole zoo.

"There's been a major ruckus there lately. Haven't you noticed that one area in the back that's all boarded up?" I said. "There must be something huge going on back there. I've heard pounding and drilling and sawing for weeks."

"You don't think it's a new dolphin act?" asked Sophie, disappointed. Dolphins are her favorite animals. I take her to the Dolphin Exploratorium every single time we visit Mom. She can't get enough of their big smiles and amazing tricks.

Todd, the dolphin trainer, is proud of the exhibit, and it is the most popular one in the whole zoo. Todd is really knowledgeable about dolphins, and he teaches them to do great tricks, like jumping through hoops. He lets Sophie feed the dolphins.

"Sorry, Soph! Maybe it'll be a gigantic python for the Herpetology House," I said hopefully. "How cool would it be to have a thirty-foot python there?"

"Pretty cool, Professor Science!" said Nicole. She always calls me that. I like my nickname because learning about science is my hobby.

The Herpetology House is another popular exhibit at the zoo, and I'm not the only one who is wild about it. Kaneesha, the animal handler there, is always busy directing tours or caring for the animals. She knows everything about all the animals there and about the habitat, which is the place where animals live.

Just last night, Sophie and I looked at my science notebook. Thanks to Todd and Kaneesha, I've filled up my science notebook with tons of animal information, and Sophie always begs me to read it to her at bedtime.

"Sophie, did you know that the largest group of reptiles is formed by lizards and snakes? There are more than 3,500 species, or kinds, of lizards and more than 2,400 snake species. Most lizards prefer warm or hot habitats. So do snakes, although one type lives north of the Arctic Circle."

"Doug," asked Sophie, "what are amphibian habitats like?"

"I know it's in here somewhere," I said, as I rustled around in my notebook. "Aha! Amphibians spend part of their lives in water and part on land, so their habitats are usually moist places, such as lakes, streams, and ponds."

"Doug, do you think I can be your helper when you become a scientist?" asked Sophie.

"Do you want to be an animal handler like Kaneesha or a trainer like Todd?"

"Either one—or else a superstar," she yawned. I laughed and closed my notebook.

I remember that conversation as if it were yesterday. Oh, that's right, it *was* yesterday!

"I thought we'd never get here," said Sophie as we arrived at the zoo. "Let's hurry and find Mom. I can't wait to hear her news."

"Still holding out for dolphin tricks?" Nicole asked.

"You never know!" laughed Sophie.

As we arrived at the zoo, we saw Mom walking with a tall, gangly man we had never seen before.

"Kids, I want you to meet Dr. Fernandez. He's a herpetologist, and he's designing a fantastic new exhibit for the zoo." We all introduced ourselves.

"Is a new animal coming to the zoo?" asked Sophie.

"Yes," said Mom. "I couldn't wait to break this news to you. Remember the Japanese giant salamander we saw at the Detroit Zoological Park last year?"

"How could we forget?" asked Nicole.

"That thing was enormous!" I added.

"I'm glad it left such a lasting impression," laughed Dr. Fernandez. "At more than five feet long and one of the largest salamanders in the world, it is an unforgettable sight, and now Lakemoor Zoo is getting its own Japanese giant salamander."

I can't believe Mom managed to keep this
a secret from us, but I guess we have been
preoccupied with the dolphin exhibit a lot lately.

"I remember that these salamanders are
endangered," I said.

"Yes," said Dr. Fernandez. "They're nearly
extinct."

"It stinked?" asked Sophie, her nose wrinkled.

"Extinct," said Dr. Fernandez, smiling. "That
means that they could all die out."

"Because the Japanese giant salamander prefers to live in dark, cool, moist places," Dr. Fernandez explained, "the new habitat will feature a pond and a cave. We're going to create a rocky grotto for our new resident. These salamanders like to hide under rocks during the daytime and come out at night. You see, like many amphibians, they live on both water and land."

"What do they eat?" asked Nicole.

"Mostly insects, fish, and worms," said Dr. Fernandez. "In fact, they have sticky tongues that help them slurp up their prey!"

"Here goes Professor Science," laughed Nicole as she noticed me busily jotting down notes.

"These are great facts!" I exclaimed.

"Here's a fact that might really intrigue you," said Dr. Fernandez. "The Japanese giant salamander has barely changed appearance in thirty million years." Dr. Fernandez invited all of us to return the next afternoon, when the concrete was going to be poured to make the foundation for the rock grotto.

"Is concrete the same thing as cement?" I inquired the next day, as we watched the workers preparing the gray concoction.

"That's an excellent question," said Rob, one of the workers. "Cement gets mixed with other ingredients to make concrete."

"You mean like the ingredients we mix together when we make cookies?" asked Sophie.

"Well, kind of," said Rob. "Cement is a very fine, gray powder. See, here's some in the bag." We drew closer for a look. "It gets mixed with water, gravel, sand, and some crushed stone to make concrete. It can be formed into any shape. Then the mixture changes and hardens. It becomes superstrong. Cement alone isn't as strong as concrete."

I rustled around in my notebook. "I knew I had some notes about cement. Dad told me all about it. The powder is made from clay and limestone, which is a sedimentary rock! When fragments from weathered rocks get compressed, they form sedimentary rock," I explained.

"That's right," said Rob, "and the ingredients we mix the powder with to make concrete are rocks too. In fact, many building materials are made from rock."

We watched as the workers dumped the thick, gray goop onto wooden planks that had been laid as supports. They used wooden spades to move the concrete right up against the planks and to press it into the corners. Then they smoothed the entire surface with a tool called a trowel.

"These will hold this foundation nice and tight," he said.

We watched as the workers covered the whole foundation with water.

"What's that for?" I wondered.

"It keeps the concrete moist so that it won't crack." Rob then covered the foundation with a wet piece of burlap to keep it from drying too quickly. I wrote quickly, recording everything.

Because the workers were going to be busy building the grotto for the next week, we spent most of our time visiting Todd at the Dolphin Exploratorium, and Sophie chattered a million miles a minute.

"Todd, a new salamander is coming! It's coming all the way from Japan, and it's huge—taller than Doug."

"Hmmm," Todd grumbled. "Kaneesha told me all about it. The Dolphin Exploratorium has been the most popular exhibit at this zoo since I was a kid. Kaneesha is gloating like crazy! She thinks everyone will scramble to the Herpetology House to see the salamander." Todd looked unhappy.

"Don't worry, Todd," said Sophie. "This will always be my favorite place in the whole zoo."

"And I'm sure we'll keep bringing her here every single day," reassured Nicole sympathetically.

Each day after school, we took a glimpse of the progress on the exhibit. A group of art students from the college in town had volunteered to make the grotto. It would have all kinds of nooks and crannies for the salamander to explore. The students arranged boulders and sealed them together with cement to create a cave. Other rocks and ledges framed the cave so that the habitat's new resident would have cool places to doze.

When Saturday came, we zipped over to the zoo with Dad. Sometimes Mom worked in the morning on Saturdays, and we all liked to stroll around the zoo together in the afternoons. Sophie had gotten Dad excited about the salamander, and we were all eager to find out about the progress being made on the exhibit. With my hand itching to do some notetaking, I could not wait to see the exhibit. Walking up to the entrance of the zoo, Sophie pulled Dad's arm, urging him to move faster.

We found Kaneesha conducting a tour. When her group thanked her and left, she joined up with our family.

"I think I can guess what you want to see," she teased. "I'll open the exhibit so that we can all see how it's going. This is so exciting!" We put some special heat lamps in here overnight so that the grotto would dry quickly. I haven't seen it since yesterday, but it was looking great then."

We all clustered around Kaneesha as she heaved open the door. Waving us in, she stepped inside, and we eagerly followed.

Suddenly, we stopped short, our mouths opened in horror, and everyone gasped. "Oh, no!" cried Sophie.

The habitat was in shambles. Heat lamps had fallen down, shattering glass on the floor and knocking down plants around the pond. The plants looked limp and lifeless.

"What on Earth . . . ?" said Dad.

"This is a crime scene!" shouted Kaneesha. "Someone has vandalized our exhibit!"

"Who would do a thing like that?" I asked in disbelief.

Mom pondered my question for a minute and said, "I have no idea—I'm baffled."

"I'm stumped too," began Nicole. "Wait a minute. Remember how Todd got irritated whenever we talked about the salamander? He wasn't exactly thrilled about it coming here, and he didn't want competition with the Dolphin Exploratorium."

"Let's not be so quick to draw conclusions," Mom cautioned us sternly. "We need to gather facts before we make any serious accusations like that."

"Well, Professor Science," said Nicole. "What are we waiting for? Let's start looking for clues to solve this mystery!" She turned her head slowly as she scanned the room.

"I don't think that will be necessary, Nicole," I said confidently. "I think I have this salamander stumper all figured out!" Everyone stared at me, and Sophie crossed her fingers. "I think I have some notes about . . . ," I said, my voice trailing off as I rustled through my notebook. "Let me just look something up."

"It was the combination of the heat lamps and the cement that made this exhibit come tumbling down," I explained. "Remember, Rob said concrete is stronger than cement. And remember what Rob did to keep the concrete moist?"

"Sure," said Nicole. "He carefully covered the foundation with water and the wet burlap."

"Very observant," I said. "That moisture kept the foundation from cracking."

"So I guess that's why the foundation is still in place," said Kaneesha.

"But I guess the students didn't know that they should use concrete rather than cement. And they also made the mistake of bringing in heat lamps to dry it." I went on. "It got way too hot in here, and heat causes water to evaporate—and much faster with cement than with concrete. Because the water evaporated, the cement became more and more dry, and it shrank very fast. It shrank until it cracked."

"And those cracks made the crash?" asked Sophie.

"You'll be my assistant in no time, Soph! Yes, the cracks caused the crash."

"Doug, you rock!" said Nicole with a smile. "Get it?" she laughed. "I guess I was wrong to blame Todd for the crash. It was really all about science."

"Well done, Doug!" said Mom, smiling. "I'm proud of the way you used what you know about science to figure out the mystery. Thank goodness the salamander hasn't arrived from Japan yet. But now that we know how to avoid this crash in the future, what can we do about the present?"

"What are we waiting for?" asked Kaneesha. "Let's get everyone back on the job and get this exhibit off the ground!"

"This exhibit is great, Mom," said Nicole a few weeks later when we joined Kaneesha and Dr. Fernandez to have a look.

The exhibit was finally about to open. The art students went back to the drawing board. This time, they used concrete and water to keep it moist as it dried. The heat lamps were removed, and the concrete held tight.

The rock grotto was perfect. It had ledges the salamander could rest on, and it had a great big opening where the giant salamander was hiding right now.

"I wish we could see him!" said Sophie.

"Keep watching. He'll come out," Mom promised. "Well, Doug, I guess we have you to thank for helping this exhibit get built again, the right way!"

"Yes," said Kaneesha. "When this opens to the public tomorrow, it's going to make a lot of people happy, especially me!"

"Oh, thanks," I said. "You know, Soph, I hope the salamander comes out too! I'm dying to fill up my notebook with facts about him!"

"I want to fill up my notebook too," said Sophie excitedly, and she held up a little notepad Mom had given her. "I can't write yet," Sophie said, "but I can draw."

"That's a great way to start recording your observations," said Mom.

"Yes, some scientists use sketches and pictures along with written notes to show details about what they are researching," said Dr. Fernandez. Sophie beamed and flashed a big smile.

"I can't wait to start!" she exclaimed.

"It will be nice to have illustrations to match up with the facts that I record too," I added.

Suddenly, Todd burst into the room. His hair was sticking out all over his head, and he looked flushed and upset.

"Professor Science," he called, out of breath. "I need your help at the Dolphin Exploratorium! A giant load of fish food is missing."

"Let's go, Sophie," I said. "This sounds like a mystery you can help me with."

# Endangered! The Japanese Giant Salamander

You've read about the ways Dr. Fernandez tried to build a great habitat for the Japanese giant salamander, but what is the state of its habitat in the wild?

As Dr. Fernandez explained, the giant Japanese salamander is an endangered animal. That means that it is at risk of becoming extinct. How did it become at risk? In the same unfortunate way that other animals have become endangered. Its habitat is being destroyed. Dams have been built across the rivers where the salamander makes its home in Japan. Forested areas that they live in are also being destroyed.

What is being done to make sure that the salamander will have a place to lay its eggs? One idea is to build dams out of stone. That way, the nooks and crannies the salamander needs will be available. It is a solution Dr. Fernandez would like!